Jefferson County Central

Urban Trails

another book in the *Take A Bike!* series

also by Glen Hanket:

Underwear by the Roadside: LitterWalk Coast-to-Coast

-- the story of Glen and his wife Susan, who spent twelve months walking from Maine to Oregon, bagging four tons of litter and discovering the 'real America'.

Take A Bike! A Guide to the Denver Area's Urban Trails (2nd Edition)

-- Winner of the 2003 CIPA Evvy Award

Trails Away Colorado: Quick Escapes for Bikes, Blades, and Boots

-- trails spanning the whole state

And the books of the *Take a Bike* series:

- **Boulder Urban Trails**
- **Broomfield-Boulder County Urban Trails**
- **Adams County Urban Trails**
- **Westminster Urban Trails**
- **Jefferson County Central Urban Trails**
- **Northern Colorado Urban Trails**
- **Mountain Resorts Urban Trails**
- **Denver/Platte Triangle Urban Trails**
- **Aurora/East Metro Urban Trails**
- **Douglas County Urban Trails**
- **Jefferson County South Urban Trails**

Jefferson County Central Urban Trails

another book in the *Take A Bike!* series

CAK Publishing _____

PO Box 953   Broomfield, CO 80038

Published by CAK Publishing, PO Box 953, Broomfield CO 80038

Catalog-in-Publication

Hanket, Glen
    Jefferson County central urban trails : another book in the take
a bike! series / by Glen Hanket. – 1st ed.
    p. cm..
    Includes index.
    ISBN: 0-9709815-6-2

    1. Bicycle touring—Colorado—Denver. 2. Bicycle
trail—Colorado—Denver. 3. Bicycle trail—Colorado—Jefferson
County. 4. Denver—Guidebooks.   I. Title.

GV1045.5.C6H36 2000   796.64'09788
                               CKI00-64067

Printed in Canada

A hearty 'Thank You' goes to

Steve Lingenfelter

Parks Superintendent in Golden

You've done a tremendous job in that city!

-- and to --

Portia Masterson

Thanks for supporting independent publishing!

-- and to --

Christopher Herron

His cover designs are the best!

T*able of Contents*

- Introduction   1

- Rules of the Road   2

- How to Use This Book   4

- Trails Overview   5

- Pomona Neighborhood Loop   7

- Little Dry Creek Trail west (Arvada)   10

- Little Dry Creek Trail east (Arvada/Adams County)   13

- Club Crest and Indian Tree Loops   17

-      Club Crest Loop   18

-      Indian Tree Loop   20

- Lake Arbor Paths (Lake and Spine)   22

- Ralston Creek Trail east   25

- Ralston Creek Trail central   28

- Ralston Creek Trail/Arvada Reservoir   31

- Ward Hill-Yankee Doodle Loop   34

- Van Bibber Creek Trail and Loop   36

- Fairmount Trail   39
- Clear Creek Trail central   43
- Clear Creek Trail west   46
- Golden City Loop   50
- Kinney Run Trail   55
- US6 Trail   57
- South Golden Rd Trail   60

Introduction

Ahhh, to spend an hour two-wheeling – what could be finer? Feeling the sun on your face and a breeze at your back, passing under a canopy of trees, listening to birds sing – at these times, the problems of the world are miles away.

But you don't need to be – miles away, that is. For the Denver metro area hosts an extensive network of bike trails. Forget about needing a full day to take a simple ride – pack a lunch, load the bikes onto the car, drive an hour into the mountains, whoops! Time to drive back already. Instead, hop on a short trail near your home, or explore one of the long trails snaking through the metroplex.

The climate in Colorado encourages sports like bicycling. Even during the dead of winter snow rarely lasts, and dry, sunny days make it easy to get your exercise without spending your time inside a club. This region has had a love affair with bikes for many years. In 1900, reported the Denver Post, the city had more bikes per residents than any other US city.

However, automobiles pushed bikes out of the spotlight, and many years passed with no emphasis on bike facilities. Isolated trails existed in widely-spaced parks, or ran a short distance along Cherry Creek, but no network existed. Then the South Platte River flooded in 1965, sparking interest in converting it from an eyesore to a public treasure – which included bike trails running its length.

In June 1974 Mayor Bill McNichols appointed Joe Shoemaker chairman of the Platte River Development Committee. With a few hand-picked members, he tackled the transformation of the river. City dumps became parks, and dams soon sported boat chutes. By mid-1975, the first segments of the Platte River had opened, followed by the dedication of Confluence Park that September.

Now twenty years have passed, and over three hundred miles of trails weave through the metropolitan area. Some offer steep pitches for a workout; others meander along lazy streams. No matter what style you prefer, there is bound to be something for you.

Before you take your ride, though, remember that biking can be dangerous. Always keep safety in mind, from the equipment you wear (yes, helmets can save lives!) to the traffic you ride in. Keep alert for pedestrians sharing your trails, and check both ways when crossing busy streets. At most major boulevards, a crossing light is available nearby.

R *ules of the Road*

So you've reached the trailhead. Now you're ready to fly down the pavement, setting a new land speed record, right?

WRONG!

One of the biggest challenges facing trail users is retaining the right to use those trails. Not everyone welcomes trails in their area, and many people actively fight to have them removed from their neighborhoods. They cite out-of-control bicyclists injuring bystanders or hikers trashing public lands as ammunition in their fight against the paths. Unless we're all careful, a few thoughtless individuals could make us lose the wonderful paths we enjoy.

To prevent that, trail users have adopted the 'rules of the road'. The ten common-sense rules:

1. Cyclists and skaters should yield to horses and hikers.

2. Cyclists and skaters should maintain control at all times. This means keeping your speed within reasonable limits, and slowing down when approaching blind curves.

3. Obey all signs and postings.

4. Respect private property. Close any gates you opened, and don't damage someone's land.

5. Wear a helmet when cycling and pads when skating.

6. Do not obstruct a path by stopping in the middle of it.

7. Always walk or ride on the right.

8. When passing someone, call out to warn them.

9. Do not litter!

10. Use extra caution when wearing headphones. You may not hear someone coming from behind.

Remember that you are sharing these paths with other users. Be an ambassador of good will! Something as simple as saying "Good morning" or "Good afternoon" as you pass someone goes a long way to brightening their day, and breaks down the stereotype of the 'rude cyclist'.

How to use this book

All trails in this book may be ridden with any type bicycle; no single- or double-track trails are included here. Most of the trails are also suitable for in-line skaters – check the 'Surface' description on the top of each writeup to insure that it is hard-surfaced. (However, some of the paved paths may be too weathered for a comfortable ride.) Of course, any of these trails are appropriate for a short walk.

In each writeup, special font styles call out convenient <u>trailheads</u> (usually city parks), *other trails*, and *on-street bike routes*.

Certain maps include symbols to describe landmarks you may pass. The symbols and meanings are:

	city hall or offices		golf course
	Gardens		parking / trailhead
	Library		hospital
	ball fields		tennis courts
	school		swimming
	post office		playground

T*rails Overview*

Jefferson County ranks as the second-most-populous county in Colorado (2000 projection), slightly smaller than Denver and gaining fast. Extending from Sheridan Blvd into the foothills, the county hosts terrain ranging from flat prairie to steep hills. Most of the people reside in the urbanized east, part of the continuous city stretching from Denver to Golden in the north.

The central part of the county, including Arvada,

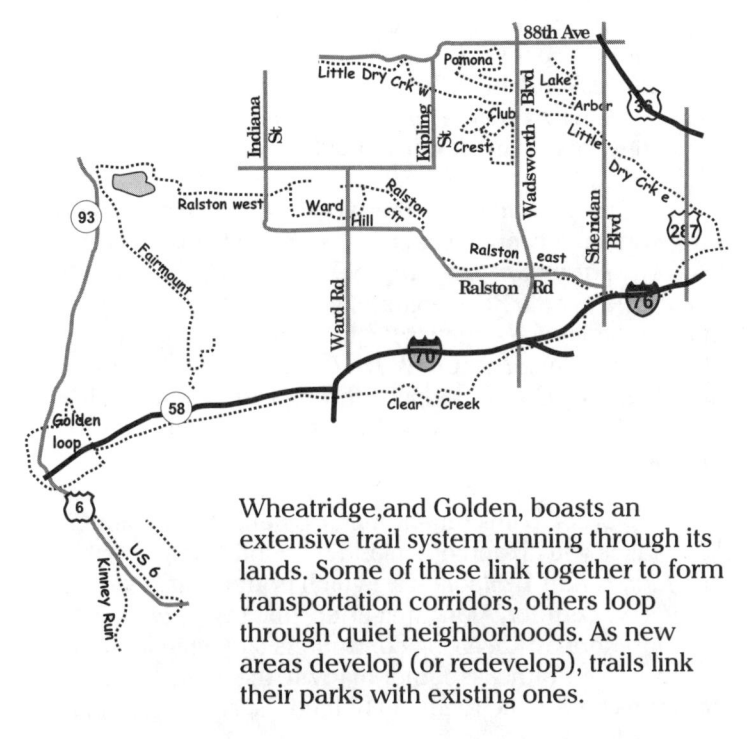

Wheatridge,and Golden, boasts an extensive trail system running through its lands. Some of these link together to form transportation corridors, others loop through quiet neighborhoods. As new areas develop (or redevelop), trails link their parks with existing ones.

The greatest concentration of trails in northern Jefferson County lie immediately west of Wadsworth Blvd near Standley Lake. On the north side, straddling the border of Westminster and Arvada, the *Pomona Neighborhood*

Loop winds back and forth around Pomona High School. South of 80th Ave, the *Club Crest* and *Indian Tree* loops visit the tracts near the Indian Tree Golf Course. The *Little Dry Creek West Trail* runs from Wadsworth west to the fringes of the suburbs. Acros the bouldevard, the *Little Dry Creek Trail East* follows the waterway downstream through older neighborhoods and greenbelts to its terminus at Clear Creek. Just north of this leg lies trails centered around *Lake Arbor*.

The region's next major creek also provides a setting for a long trail. The *Ralston Creek East Trail* runs from its mouth at Clear Creek upstream past Old Town Arvada. *Ralston Creek Central Trail* visits the neighborhoods of central Arvada, running through the grounds of the Apex Center. *Ralston Creek West* eventually leaves the city for a strenuous ride above Arvada Reservoir. The *Ward Hill/Yankee Doodle Trail* provided a Ralston trail link before the Apex Center opened, and still provides the basis for a loop ride/workout in western Arvada.

Along Arvada's southern border, the *Van Bibber Trail* runs from county open space to the sports fields at 58th and Oak. The *Fairmount Trail* runs beside North Table Mountain, linking the Arvada Reservoir trail almost to Clear Creek. Of course, the central county's largest creek has trails running alongside it. The *Clear Creek Trail Central* takes the cyclist from Little Dry Creek to Kipling through an at-times lush greenbelt, while *Clear Creek Trail West* now runs all the way into Golden.

Several paths run through Golden. The *Golden City Loop* takes you up and down and hills and along the creek. The *Kinney Run Trail* follows a gulch from Heritage Square to the US6 corridor. Along that artery, the *US6 Trail* runs from 19th St to Rooney Rd, giving commuters a chance to avoid traffic. In the northeast corner of town, the*South Golden Rd Trail* runs beside the road and behind the strip malls on its way to Ulysses Park.

Pomona Neighborhood Loop

DISTANCE:	_3.7 mile loop, 2.3 off-street_
ON-STREET:	_residential streets_
SURFACE:	_concrete, crushed gravel_
DIFFICULTY:	_easy ride_

DESCRIPTION:

Westminster and Arvada share a long city border. They also share a penchant for bike paths running through their residential areas, and the tracts west of Wadsworth Blvd boast their share of the access routes. From Countryside on the north to Indian Tree on the south, the paths tie together a built-up section of the north Denver metro area. In the Pomona Lake area, you can tour a bit of both cities on a back-and-forth loop.

We'll describe this tour starting in Westminster's Nottingham Park at 87th Dr and Allison Dr, at the covered pavilion. Follow the crushed gravel path west beside a swale choked with brush and wild grass. You quickly enter a groomed corridor of open space, with the trail surface becoming concrete and the ditch now encased in concrete. Cross Dover St (0.2) into Trailside Park, a site equipped with playground and picnic tables. Scattered trees provide a counterpoint to the grassy park.

At mile 0.5, exit the park by turning right on _86th Ave_. Follow it to its end at _Garrison St_. On Garrison turn left, entering Arvada. This street ends quickly also (at mile 0.9), and you turn right onto _Hoyt Wy/84th Ave_. Keep alert! because the trail forms very quickly on your left before you reach the next street.

At first the trail is nothing more than a sidewalk tightly hugged by privacy fences on either side. Quickly, though, the trail enters <u>Rainbow I Park</u>, a large park with basketball courts, numerous picnic tables, and a playground for the little ones (or for adults who feel like swinging). There are a few options on paths to ride through the park,

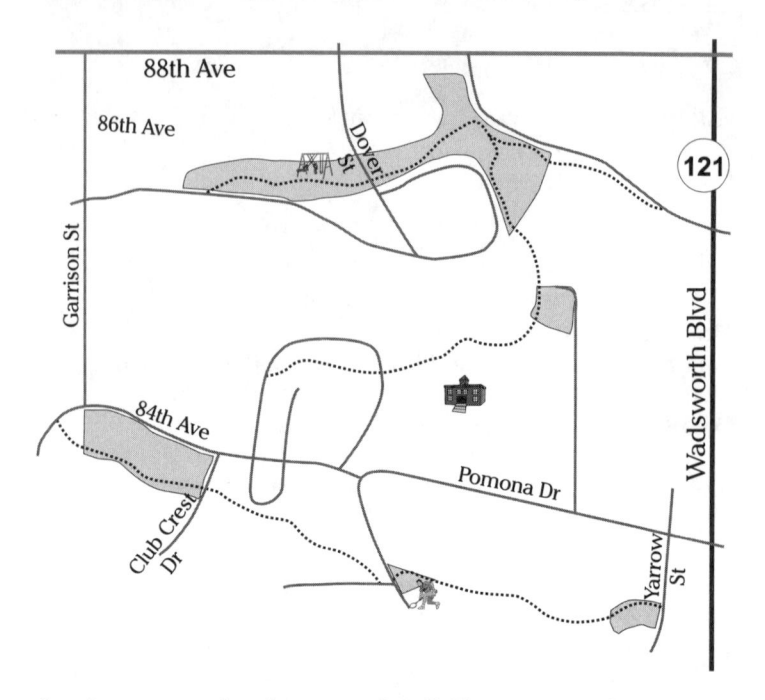

but I suggest using the central trail. The canopy of trees provides shade as well as a pleasant atmosphere.

However you get there, work your way to the southeast corner of the park (1.3). Here you cross Club Crest Dr into another strip between houses. Don't worry, this path won't stir up your claustrophobia. After a short, narrow run, the trail enters another park behind Weber Elementary School (1.5). At mile 1.7 the path joins 81st Pl and quickly crosses Pomona Dr into <u>Rainbow II Park</u>, which features a playground and tennis courts. The trail continues past the tennis courts into another house-bordered strip, emerging into <u>Rainbow III Park</u> at mile 2.0. Head left at the fork, and finish this trail when it ends at *Yarrow St* (2.1).

Head left on Yarrow and left again on the next street, *Pomona Dr* (2.2). This road, probably the most heavily trafficked in this area (but still not terribly busy), is great to bicycle on. This nice parkway has wide bike lanes on either side to keep you away from the cars. Follow it to the end of the parkway (past Pomona High School), and when Pomona makes a 140° turn, go straight instead on *84th Ave* (2.7). Take the fourth right turn from here onto *Dudley Ct/84th Cir* at mile 2.9. This street takes you to another bike path on your right (3.1).

Again you are riding through a narrow strip between houses. You will cross 84th Cir at mile 3.2 before passing behind the athletic fields attached to Pomona High School. At mile 3.5 you reach Westree Park (hosting a playground) and a trail leading to the street. Instead of going to the street, head left onto a crushed gravel path and re-enter Westminster. This path returns you to your starting point at the pavilion. If you're not quite ready to quit riding, you can cruise down the spur that runs east into the rest of Nottingham Park. It follows the gully we started next to, ending just 0.3 miles later at Yukon St.

TRAIL OPTION:

If you take Dover St north across 88th, you quickly come to Dover Square Park. A bridge in the northwest corner of the park provides access to the *Standley Center Loop* (see *Westminster Urban Trails* for more details).

Little Dry Creek Trail west (Arvada)

DISTANCE: *3.7 miles, 3.1 off-street*

ON-STREET: *residential streets*

SURFACE: *concrete*

DIFFICULTY: *easy ride, fairly flat*

DESCRIPTION:

Standley Lake, nestled between Arvada and Westminster, is one of the larger reservoirs in the Denver metro area. Though there are no trails circling the lake, the neighborhoods surrounding it are laced with a web of trails. The longest one, though not continuous, is Arvada's Little Dry Creek.

The longer stretch of trail runs through the Pomona Lake and Wood Run neighborhoods of the city. This portion begins at 80th Pl and Pomona Dr, just west of Wadsworth Blvd. As the trail heads west, a line of trees in the creek bed separates it from the noise and traffic on 80th Ave.

At 0.3 miles the trail rises to Pomona Lake. Though the trail continues on either side of the lake, the left fork is recommended; the right, which borders the houses lining the lake, becomes much narrower and is limited to pedestrians. The trails merge at the west end (0.5), entering a greenbelt that sandwiches the creek. The creek, very tame at this point, slowly grows wild as the trail proceeds upstream. First the boulders hemming it in disappear; as it swings around <u>Wood Run Park</u> (0.9) native vegetation shows up; and it enters a wildlife area after crossing under Kipling (1.3).

Crossing Kline St at 1.4 miles, the trail enters groomed <u>Lakecrest Park</u>. Two branches loop around the park, merging near the canal in the park's northwest corner.

A dirt path follows the canal for a very short distance before crossing over it and joining Moore St at 1.8 miles. Follow *Moore St* north, and quickly turn left on a short connector (1.9) to *Moore Ct*. Again, a short connector on your left (2.0) quickly takes you to the western portion of *83rd Pl*.

Head west on *83rd*, and left on *Newcombe St* when 83rd ends. Follow this until hitting the tennis courts at 2.3 miles. Join the trail as it heads through <u>Michael Northey Park</u>, regaining the creek and a sense of wilderness as trees line the trail.

Cross Simms St at mile 2.7 (there is a crosswalk light), and enter a tamed open space where the

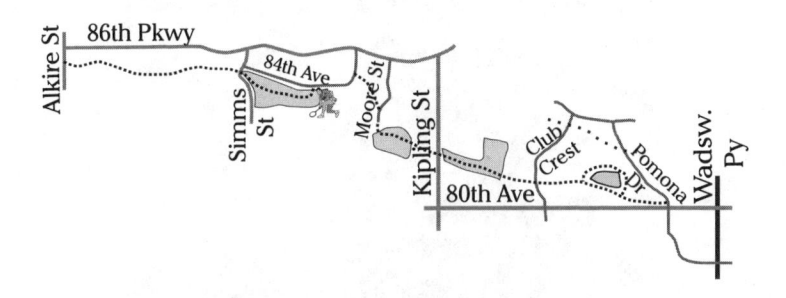

predictability of the trail matches that of the characterless, one-style-fits-all, muted-color condos that hem it in. The creek itself runs through a small concrete-lined bed, surrounded by well-kept lawns and a few strategically-place trees. To its credit, though, as the neighborhood matures, more and more flower beds and landscaped lawns decorate it. The trail crosses three quiet residential streets before gradually climbing to its end at Alkire St at the 3.7 mile mark.

TRAIL OPTIONS:

An eastern extension of the *Little Dry Creek Trail* starts at Vance Dr just south of 80th, about a half-mile east of this trail. The easiest way to reach this (and avoid the traffic on Wadsworth and 80th) is to cross 80th at the traffic light at Pomona, which becomes *Allison Wy*. Turn left on *Allison St*, which curves to become *77th Dr*. Take this across Wadsworth (again, a traffic light makes this easy), and follow it as it curves north (becoming *Vance Dr*) to the trail start. This connecting route runs for 0.8 miles.

Head north on Pomona Dr (mile 0.0) or Club Crest Dr (0.7) to intersect with the *Pomona Lakes Trail*.

Head south on Club Crest Dr to find the *Club Crest* and *Indian Tree loops*.

A cyclist cruises on Ralston Creek

L*ittle Dry Creek Trail east (Arvada/Adams County)*

DISTANCE:	*4.5 miles, 4.4 off-street*
SURFACE:	*concrete*
DIFFICULTY:	*easy ride*

DESCRIPTION:

The northern metro area boasts a good number of creek trails, accessing green areas in the midst of the city. All of those trails have had significant work done in the past few years. In many cases, that work has connected disjoined sections of trail. Work along Little Dry Creek, while not connecting the two separate links, has linked the downstream portion to Clear Creek.

The Little Dry Creek Trail (do not confuse this with the like-named stream near Greenwood Village in Arapahoe County) is perhaps the least-known of north Jefferson County's waterway trails. Cutting a gully south of Standley Lake, it flows southeast to empty into Clear Creek. A path following the creek runs nearly eight miles, upstream to Alkire St near Standley Lake. However, the stream goes underground as it bypasses the busy intersection of Wadsworth Blvd and 80th Ave, diving under the strip malls covering the corner.

Start the eastern half of the trail on Vance St south of 80th. The trail joins the gully as it heads east, running through a greenbelt bordered first by businesses, then by houses. You quickly cross Webster Wy (0.1) and Pierce St (0.4), riding by the trees and brush that accompany the creek. The stream here has been lined with rocks to control erosion.

Across Pierce, you enter <u>Little Dry Creek Park</u>, a neighborhood spot with playground, basketball court, and a

13

baseball backstop without base paths. Continue downstream through the open space, crossing Marshall St at mile 0.6 and Harlan St at mile 1.0. (Were the trail builders schizophrenic? Why do they make you cross to the opposite side of the creek every time you hit a street?) Across

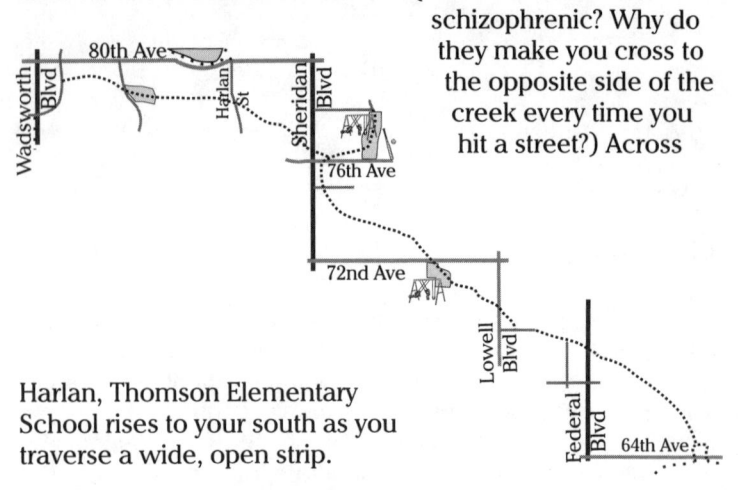

Harlan, Thomson Elementary School rises to your south as you traverse a wide, open strip.

At mile 1.2 ignore the spur to your left, which connects to Chase Cr. As you look ahead, the creek disappears – or so it seems. It actually enters a concrete gutter hidden by the tall grass. With no brush or trees to mark its path, you may think you've lost it. Follow the path as it swings south through the wild, wide grassy expanse, bearing left at mile 1.4 and quickly crossing under Sheridan Blvd (1.5). On the far side, ignore the first left branch, then turn left when the trail 'T's (1.6).

For a detour, you can climb to the street by turning right, then looping back east along the sidewalk on the north side of 76th. It soon veers from the street, running past baseball diamonds to <u>Wolff Run Park</u>, complete with a playground, basketball and tennis courts, and picnic pavilions. This spur ends at 78th Ave and Wolff St at mile 2.0.

The main trail continues under 76th, then turns sharply (watch your speed) to cross the creek as it runs along a concrete flood way. After passing 75th Ave (1.8) the trail climbs back up to street level into <u>Kennedy Park</u>, a wide grassy strip. Far to the side, condos line the open space.

Enjoy this bit of greenery, because the terrain is about to change. At mile 2.0 the trail descends again into the concrete spillway, following the caged stream under streets. Above you, back yards perch above the canal. On the concrete walls of the spillway, you can see the results of the constant war between the graffiti artists and those who paint it over.

Cross under 72nd Ave at mile 2.5 into <u>England Park</u> (playground here). You have now left behind the concrete straightjacket enclosing the creek. Rocks again line the waterway to control its course. Proceed through a strip that begins to narrow. Soon you'll reach a site you may not have expected – a firefighter's training center (2.8). If it's in use, you may want to stop and watch the exercises. When you continue you'll pass under Lowell Blvd (3.0) into the trail's wildest stretch , filled with trees and brush.

The trail quickly dumps you onto 69th Ave. You can call this the end of your ride (mile 3.1), or you can brave a short, rough stretch to continue. If you choose to go forth, head left on the road. It quickly turns into a rough, rutted dirt lane before reaching the last concrete section of trail (3.2). At mile 3.4 you cross the extension of Grove St, and pass under Federal Blvd at mile 3.5. Here is the newest stretch of concrete, taking you under the railroad tracks before rising again. This is not particularly scenic - to the north industry intrudes, and the rails follow you on the south. If not for the trees along the creek, you could forget you're following a waterway.

At mile 4.2 the trail forks: to the left a trail leads to batting cages on 64th Ave, where a tunnel under the street connects to the eastern portion of the *Clear Creek Trail*. The official trail heads right, under the tracks (4.3), and past a wild stretch of creek choked with vegetation. It quickly crosses under 64th to join the central section of the *Clear Creek Trail* (4.5).

Connect with the western stretch of the _Little Dry Creek Trail_ by taking _Vance Dr_ south (which becomes _77th Dr_), crossing Wadsworth at the light, and winding north onto _Allison St_ and _Wy_, crossing 80th Ave at the light. On the north side this is Pomona St, where the trail quickly begins.

Ride the eastern or central sections of the _Clear Creek Trail_. Note that there is only a short section of unimproved social trail directly connecting the two legs, and a detour on the lower legs is recommended for linking the two.

*C*lub Crest and Indian Tree Loops

The Club Crest neighborhood in Arvada, southwest of Wadsworth Blvd and 80th Ave, serves as the southern edge for the bike paths weaving through the neighborhoods off Wadsworth. From 108th Ave and the Countryside trail south to Indian Tree Golf Course, the trails tie together the housing tracts in the suburbs of Arvada and Westminster. This neighborhood hosts two short loops (Club Crest and Indian Tree), which can easily be tied together for a longer ride.

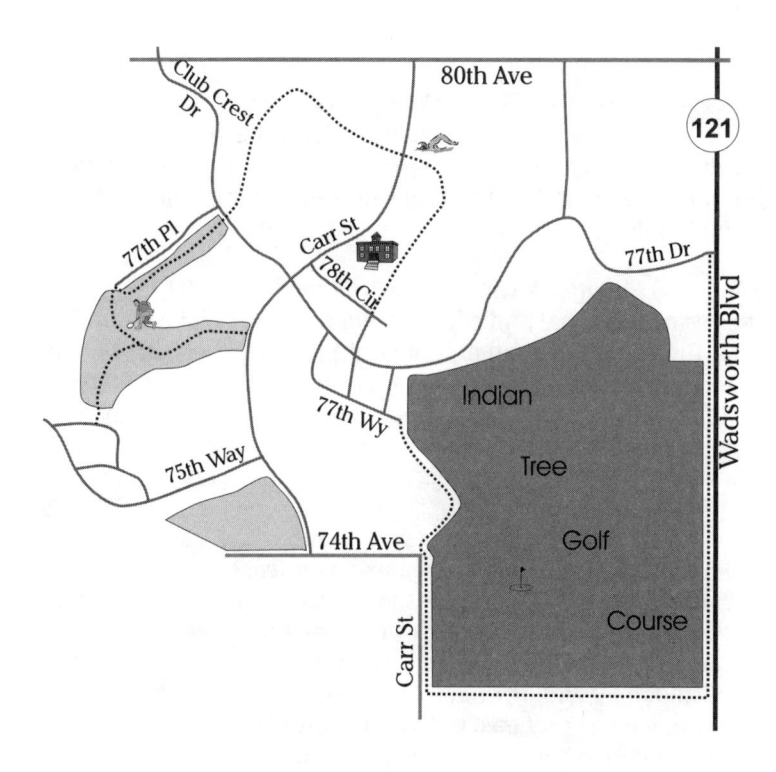

Club Crest Loop

DISTANCE: 1.6 miles, 1.3 off-street

ON-STREET: residential streets

SURFACE: concrete

DIFFICULTY: easy ride

DESCRIPTION:

This loop, the more western of the pair, stays entirely within the Club Crest tract. It tours residential areas and parks.

Start this trail in <u>Club Crest North Park</u> where it ends at Carr Dr, south of Everett Wy. This groomed park starts at the level of the canal running through it, but quickly drops into a grassy expanse highlighted by tennis and basketball courts, soccer fields, and a playground. As the trail passes the tennis courts, the park widens significantly.

At mile 0.2 you reach a trail fork. The left branch crosses the canal and climbs quickly to the neighborhoods on the south. You can detour your bike past the steps on the trail, but beware of them if you enter the park this way – the slope of the trail can give you a good head of speed, and the steps may be hidden until it's almost too late to avoid them. If you choose to ride on this path, exercise caution.

Continue straight, staying north of the canal as you pedal through the rest of the park. You will cross Club Crest Dr (0.5) as the trail continues in a grassy strip surrounding a small gully. Houses line the open space on either side. At mile 0.8 the trail hits a 'T' intersection, with the left branch immediately ending on a side street. Turn right instead, heading east-southeast between Everett and 79th Ave. This portion of the trail ends when you return to Carr Dr (1.0).

Across the street lies Meyers Swimming Center and Warder Elementary School. Cross to the swim center and follow the trail behind it, which then veers right to pass between the school and apartments across a ditch. Take this path until it ends on a quiet cul de sac (1.3). Turn left on *Brentwood Ct*, then right on the first street (*Club Crest East*). As you climb this slight grade, you are treated to a magnificent view of Longs Peak ahead of you. Turn left again on *Carr Ct* (1.4), which curves around to *Carr Dr* and your starting point in the park (1.5).

<u>*TRAIL OPTIONS:*</u>

To connect with the *Indian Tree Loop*, take *Brentwood* straight another block, where it ends on 77*th Wy*. Go left on 77th to the end to find the *Indian Tree Trail*.

Head north on Club Crest Dr across 88th Ave to reach the *Little Dry Creek West Trail* or, a bit further, the *Pomona Neighborhood Loop.*

Overlooking Indian Hills Golf Course

19

I*ndian Tree Loop*

DISTANCE: *2.4 mile loop, 1.6 off-street*

ON-STREET: *residential streets*

SURFACE: *concrete, blacktop*

DIFFICULTY: *easy to moderate ride*

DESCRIPTION:

This trail differs greatly from its partner, the Club Crest Loop. For much of its length it avoids the neighborhoods, circling the golf course and cruising down the Wadsworth trail. The scenery is as pleasant if not nicer, though, surrounded by the greenery of the golf course.

Start this trail at the eastern end of 77th Way. A cement trail waits at the end of the street, taking you between the open expanses of Indian Tree Golf Course and the meandering canal. Older trees line the bank here and there, providing shade on hot days. You pass by a pond on the Indian Tree grounds, and then by cascade pools gurgling down a landscaped slope. Not a bad setting for a round of golf.

Follow the trail as it parallels Carr St (not the Carr Dr mentioned in the Club Crest Loop), then turn east sharply at mile 0.5 to stay on the perimeter of the golf course. The trail becomes a rough blacktop path squeezed between the course and smaller, older homes. It parallels a small drainage ditch, and the houses sport little bridges to connect their well-kept back yards with the trail. Again, established trees help to provide shade, as well as a carpet of leaves on the trail in the fall.

At mile 1.0 the trail hits Wadsworth Blvd. Follow it to the left/north, as it quickly descends the hill into the Little Dry Creek drainage. The trail is well-kept, but keep an eye on your speed – there are driveways with traffic in and out of the golf course, and you don't want to surprise a driver that just triple-bogeyed hole 18. The land levels out by the time you reach the Indian Tree Mall (1.5), a strip mall on your left. You may choose to ride through the mall parking lot, or follow the Wadsworth Trail until you hit *77th Dr*. In both cases, turn left on 77th and pedal past the post office, reaching *Allison Wy* at mile 1.9.

Turn left here, and gear down as you climb up part of the hill you just descended. Thankfully, this hill seems less steep than the downhill you flew down on the Wadsworth Trail. After cresting the hill, look for the bike route sign, and turn left on *Brentwood St* (2.4). It ends in one block on 77th Way, where you turn left to find your starting point.

TRAIL OPTION:

To connect with the *Club Crest Loop*, take *Allison Wy* one block past Brentwood St to Brentwood Ct. This is where the other trail joins your street (which has turned from Allison into Club Crest East).

OTHER ATTRACTIONS:

Lying south of Indian Tree on Wadsworth, the ARVADA CENTER hosts events year-round. Plays, conventions, and other features attract visitors from throughout the Denver area.

Lake Arbor Paths (Lake and Spine)

DISTANCE: 1.3 and 2.2 mile loops, mostly off-street

ON-STREET: residential streets

SURFACE: concrete

DIFFICULTY: easy ride, fairly flat

DESCRIPTION:

The Lake Arbor and Far Horizon tracts occupy the 'stretched' square mile bounded by 88th Ave, 80th Ave, Wadsworth Blvd, and Sheridan Blvd. Anchored by Lake Arbor and the like-named golf course, this area is filled with solid middle-class homes free of the uniform look of the newer, cracker-box developments sprouting like prairie weeds. Little traffic plies the streets, making it easy to connect different trail segments for loop trips. In particular, trails here lend themselves to two separate, short loops: one around the lake, another through the neighborhoods. Try either one, or do them both for a great family ride.

Spine Path and Loop – From the parking lot on the east end of lake (at the end of Pomona Dr), the spine loop leaves the lake to run north along the separating line between the Lake Arbor and Far Horizons tracts. The trail was recently resurfaced, and now provides a smooth ride as it follows a ditch filled with reeds and other wetland growth. Soon a concrete lining cuts off most of the flora, just before the trail crosses Chase Dr (0.2).

You are now riding through the edge of Far Horizons Park, adjacent to Parr Elementary School. To your left, privacy fences continue to border the trail. At mile 0.3 the trail forks – keep riding straight ahead (we'll return via the side path) as you leave the ditch behind. The trail corridor now runs due north through a grassy 'canyon' defined by the tall privacy fences on either side.

The Spine Path ends at mile 0.8 when it dumps onto *86th Ave*. To convert this into a loop trip, turn left on 86th, and follow it as it curves around. When it ends, turn right on *Lamar Dr*, and take the next left onto *Otis Dr*. (Traffic on these side streets should give you no problem.) Shortly after passing Little Elementary School (1.3), look on your left for the side spur of the Spine Path.

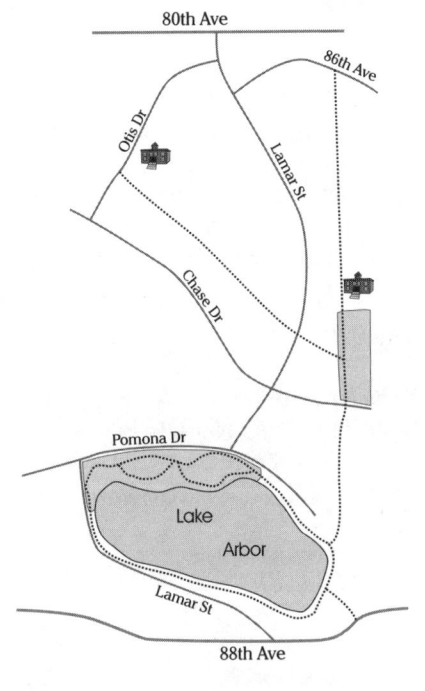

Turn left on this path for a nice treat. This narrow strip, caged by privacy fences, is well-populated with trees and brush. The greenery provides a calming effect, and the shade is a godsend on hot summer days. Unfortunately, this leg doesn't last near long enough. After crossing Lamar (1.7), enjoy one last gasp of the greenery before you merge with the main Spine Path in the park you saw earlier (1.8). Turn right here to return to the lake and the parking area (2.2).

Lake Arbor Loop – We'll describe riding this loop starting from the same parking lot at the end of Pomona Dr. The total length of the loop is 1.3 miles, with minor variations based on taking an inner or outer path on the north shore.

Being a loop trip, you can of course ride it in either direction. I recommend going clockwise, since I feel that the mountain views are better from the south side of the lake.

Not many directions are required here – keep the lake to your right! After passing by the east end, the trail squeezes between the lake and nearby condos. Soon the houses retreat across Lamar St, and you ride between the lake and the street. Watch for great Front Range views ahead of you!

On the lake's west end, geese have taken over the pavilions. Watch for them here, they can get surly. Fountains in the northwest corner provide a diversion; you can stop to watch them or press on. As you again head east, the path splits, giving you options of riding closer to shore or nearer the street. All paths quickly join again, and you ride along the lake's edge again before returning to the parking area.

TRAIL OPTION:

From the southeast corner of the lake, a 0.1 mile trail segment drops south to 80th Ave. Cross 80th onto *Harlan St* and follow it one block south to the *Little Dry Creek Trail east*.

Ralston Creek Trail east

DISTANCE: *3.2 or 3.8 miles, 3.1 off-street*

ON-STREET: *quiet residential streets*

SURFACE: *concrete*

DIFFICULTY: *easy ride, mostly flat*

DESCRIPTION:

The Denver area is home to several premier creek trails: Cherry Creek, Bear Creek, and Clear Creek are probably the best known. However, lesser-known Ralston Creek has scenery that compares with any of them, and has comparable mileage. The eastern section, through the heart of Arvada, strings together many small parks as it runs through 'downtown'.

The trail branches off from the Clear Creek Trail just west of Sheridan, as it crosses the Clear Creek on what at least one bicyclist has described as "the most beautiful bike path bridge in the metro area." I find it hard to argue - the span is elegant and graceful (and very new). On the north side, the trail cuts through Gold Strike Park, where Arvada was born. The city has built a new trailhead with parking spots and a port-a-potty on 56th Ave to access the trail.

The trail jumps into a wild stretch of land below the new Ralston Rd to the north. After passing under Ralston (0.8) and Lamar St (0.9), follow the trail up to street level. Just before reaching the sidewalk on Ralston, bear right to stay on the creek path. We'll cross over the creek where Nolan St turns into 58th Pl, on the fringes of an industrial district (1.0).

Cross Pierce St (watch for traffic) at mile 1.2 into Creekside Park, an older park bordered by apartments. The trail, more weathered here, crosses the creek three times

25

quickly before tunneling under Wadsworth Pkwy and dumping you onto *60th Ave* at Secrest Dr (1.5). (The signs must be schizo - they state, "Trail ends – this way to trail.")

This quiet street lasts only one block, but a connecting walk at the end crosses the creek and connects it to the upper block of *60th*. Ride down that street and cross Old Wadsworth Blvd (1.8) onto *Marilyn Jean Dr* and into Memorial Park. The trail begins again quickly on your left.

This established park is delightful to cruise through, with a large complement of shade trees. As you cross to the south side of the creek, watch for Disc Golf (a.k.a. Frisbee Golf) players – the park's course attracts throngs of them on nice days. At 2.1 miles, when you reach a playground, cross the creek again to leave the park, and parallel the street until passing under Carr St (2.4). The trail enters Hoskinson Park, crossing the creek again (2.6). After passing the heart of the park, the location of the picnic pavilions, municipal pool, and tennis courts, the trail crosses the creek again at mile 2.7 to leave North Jeffco Community Park (note: this turn and the next one are easy to miss on the return trip).

At 2.9 miles the trail crosses Garrison St at a light, then veers right with the creek at 3.0 miles. Cross back over

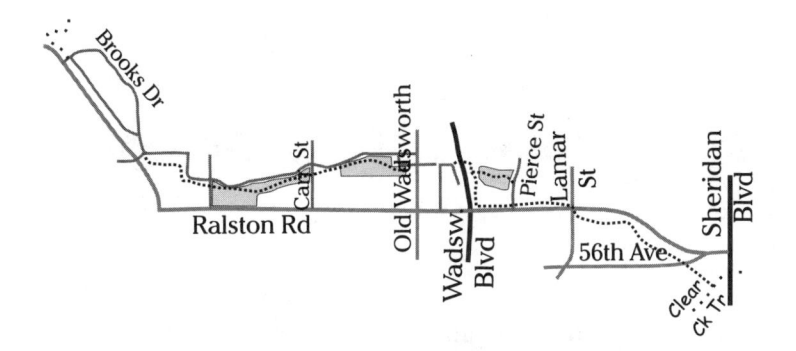

the creek and turn right (missing this turn on your return takes you into Arvada Square Shopping Center). You're now pedaling through Ralston Cove Park, a wide greenbelt filled with trees, trails and a playground, bordered by an apartment complex to your left. This path ends at 3.2 miles, dumping you onto Brooks Dr.

You may connect this stretch of the Ralston Creek Trail with the center section by a short ride through another quiet neighborhood. Continue on *Brooks Dr* and take a left onto *Johnston Way*, following it to the end (passing one stop sign along the way) and turning left again onto *Brooks*. The trail restarts at the corner of Brooks and Ralston (3.8).

Ralston Creek Trail central

DISTANCE: 2.8 miles off-street

ON-STREET: cross Ward Rd at light

SURFACE: concrete

DIFFICULTY: easy ride, flat

DESCRIPTION:

Ralston Creek runs through the center of Arvada, draining land ranging from golf courses to parking lots. A series of greenbelts and parks line the stream through almost its entire length, and a long trail uses those lands to knit the city together. The central section, linking 'downtown' in the east and golf course tracts in the west, provides perhaps the most pleasant stretch of this trail.

If you wish to connect this path with the eastern-most section, you must ride 0.6 miles through a quiet residential tract. From the eastern trail's end, go straight on *Brooks Dr* and quickly take a left on *Johnston Way*. Follow Johnston past nice homes until it ends on *Brooks* again. Turn left on Brooks, and hop on the sidewalk when you reach Ralston Rd (0.5). Take the concrete to the right at Miller St, and you will then see the trail continue on your right (0.6). Now reset your odometer.

From Miller St just north of Ralston Rd, hop on the trail as it curves towards the gentle stream. It nearly executes a U-turn, swinging back to the street. Cross Miller at 0.3 (a pedestrian light is available) and enter Oak Park, next to Campbell Elementary School (watch for this turn on the way back, also). Trees line the creek thickly, providing shade on morning rides. After crossing Oak St at 0.7 (there is a traffic light at the end of the parking lot), the corridor narrows as it passes several back yards. The route joins 68th *Ave* (0.9) and heads west (left), then quickly goes north (right) on *Pierson* and enters Davis Lane Park on another paved path.

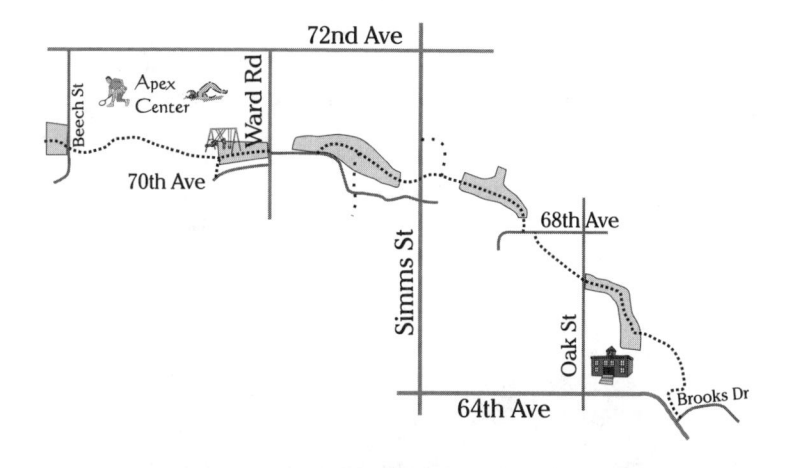

The parkland following the creek now grows quite wide, lending a relaxed feel to the ride. Ignore the short spur that branches right at 1.1 miles; it only leads into the neighborhood. After passing a small pond, we pass the *Leyden Creek Trail* at 1.4 miles (right branch) and cross under Simms St at 1.4. This stretch has a few less trees, but doesn't last long. At mile 1.8 the *Ward Hill Trail* takes off to the left; our trail crosses the bridge and continues in <u>Danny Kendricks Park</u>. The trail soon dumps onto *70th Ave*, and crosses Ward Rd (ped signal) at 2.1. The trail begins again, running beside a playground and tennis courts.

At mile 2.3, you enter the newest stretch of trail, through a large tract that had been a farm only a few years earlier. The trail, exposed to the sun, crosses the creek twice, putting you behind Westminster's Apex Center. You may reach this large recreation center by turning right at the next junction (2.6); the trail continues across the creek on your left. Follow it across Beech St into <u>Ralston Valley Park</u>, where this segment 'ends' at the main park juction (2.8).

Connect to the Ward Hill/Ralston Creek Loop by staying on the south side of the creek, then heading south along _Eldridge St._ If you wish to explore further west, stay on the creek trail as it passes under Eldridge.

Turn right onto _Leyden Creek_. This trail joins the street at Simms. You may then follow _Simms_ to 72nd and catch the path west, or cross Simms onto _71st Ave_, turn right on _71st Dr_, and turn right on _Union_. Leyden Creek begins again at 72nd and Union and runs to Leyden Park. Either route runs about one mile.

R*alston Creek Trail/Arvada Reservoir*

DISTANCE: *6.6 miles, 6.4 off-street*

ON-STREET: *short residential street*

SURFACE: *concrete*

DIFFICULTY: *flat on east end, big climbs on west*

DESCRIPTION:

One of the Denver area's steeper bike trails travels the hills around Arvada Reservoir. Drivers heading north from Golden on Highway 93 are bound to notice the trail climbing the slope above the lake in a series of steep switchbacks. They may not realize that the path leaves the open space to connect with the Ralston Creek Trail as it heads into the city.

The Ralston Creek trail runs all the way from Arvada Reservoir to Clear Creek. We'll start logging mileage on this western portion from the main junction inside Arvada's Ralston Valley Park. Follow the path under Eldridge, heading west out of the park. The landscape grows wilder as it cuts through Shadow Mountain Park, and has a particularly untamed feel after crossing under 69th Pl. The trail meanders much like the creek, crossing and re-crossing it. As you near the Indiana St underpass (0.7), a farm with weathered house and barn to the south lends an old-west aura to the area. You could probably imagine yourself a hundred miles away ... if not for the houses crowding the trail to the north.

The wilderness feel of the trail next fights the presence of industrial buildings on each side, followed by a large lot with piles of dirt that looks ripe for development (as of early 2000). At 1.2 miles it enters Westwoods Ranch Golf Course, a band of trees and wild growth (and "Wildlife Habitat — Stay on Trail" signs) separating well-groomed golf

31

holes on either side. Cross the creek after the "Golf Course Ahead" sign (2.0) — going straight puts you on the golf cart path — and follow West Woods Cir until the trail passes under Quaker St (2.2). (Don't take the bridge over the creek here — again, it's for the golf carts.)

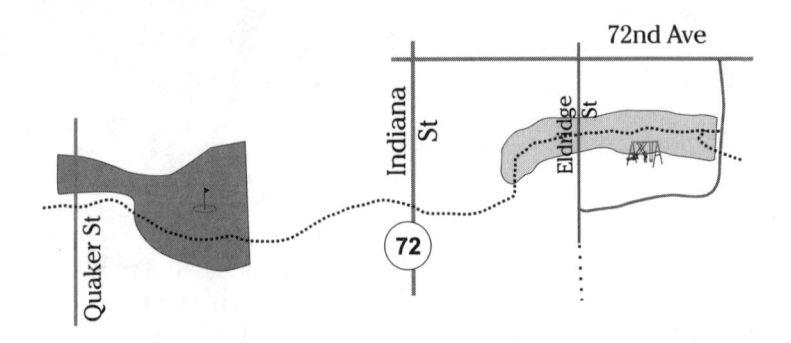

On the other side the trail climbs again to the sidewalk then cuts back to cross over the creek at Quaker St — be careful not to go forward along West Woods. The trail crosses the golf course before dropping back down to the creek. Wildlife habitat resumes as the brush grows so profuse it is difficult to see the creek. To your right country-club mega-condos line the open space. At 2.9 miles the *Ralston Creek Trail* abruptly ends where a new 9-hole golf course is being built. Join *Torrey St* as it ascends a short, steep hill, and turn left on *70th Ave* at the top (3.1). A gravel path quickly starts on your left, becoming the *Arvada Reservoir Trail* at 3.3 miles.

Houses are now behind you as you enter the reservoir area. The trail turns one switchback then climbs north above Tucker Lake. After another 2½ switchbacks, the trail straightens out (4.0) — but don't relax yet. Another mile of steep then shallow climbing follows before reaching a knoll above Arvada Reservoir. To the southeast you can see the skyscrapers of downtown Denver, to the southwest Highway 93 winds along the foothills — and ahead of you the trail slices down the hillside in six long cuts (all but the first two out of sight beneath the slope's curve).

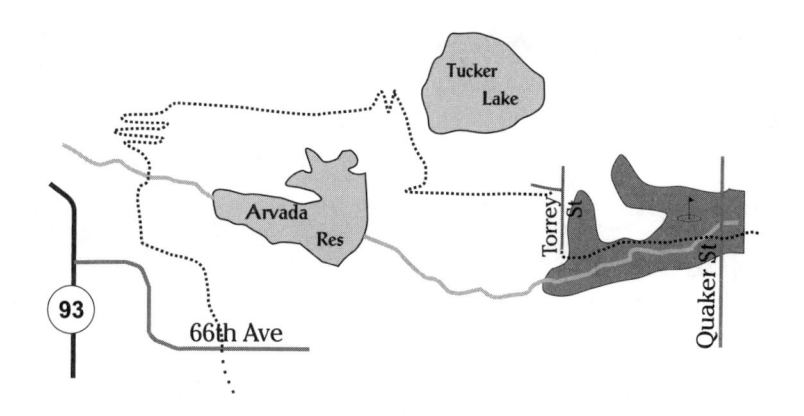

After coasting down the hill (and working your brakes), cruise north and west of the reservoir as the trail circles through the wild parkland to end at 66th Ave. Take a well-deserved rest now, before climbing the switchbacks as you return along the same trail.

TRAIL OPTIONS:

Take the *Ward Hill/Ralston Creek Loop* by cycling south on Eldridge St, which eventually connects to the central portion of the Ralston Creek Trail, which you can ride back to your starting point.

Take the tunnel under 66th Ave and ride south on the dirt and gravel *Fairmount Trail* as it winds along the base of North Table Mountain.

Ward Hill-Yankee Doodle Loop

DISTANCE: *2.6 miles, 1.9 off street*

ON-STREET: *uncontrolled crossing of Ward Rd*

SURFACE: *concrete*

DIFFICULTY: *steep trail over Ward Hill*

DESCRIPTION:

Until early 2002, the Ralston Creek trail had a large gap where the Apex center now stands. However, there are trails that allowed the thru-rider to link eastern and western halves with only a short stretch on-street. Those trails now allow the cyclist to execute a loop ride in the central section of the creek, using those trails along with the new link behind the Apex Center.

The connector leaves *Ralston Creek Center Trail* at the bridge crossing into Danny Kendricks Park East. It crosses 68th St and hits switchbacks as it climbs the steep Ward Hill. Late 2003 saw this area being redeveloped, with new roads added and brand new building in the midst of the turns – it looks like a public facility, but was too early to tell. The trail finishes the hill on *Union St*, reaching the top at 0.5 miles. Stay on the path to reach *Union St* at 67th Ave, on the opposite side of the hill. Cruise down Union to its end, turn right on *65th Pl*, left on *Urban St* and right on *65th Dr* to reach Ward Rd (0.9).

Be careful of crossing Ward Rd; traffic is often heavy. (If you prefer, you can catch the traffic light south of here at Ralston Rd.) On the other side, *65th* ends in two blocks (1.1). The *Yankee Doodle Trail* continues straight onto the grounds of Stott Elementary School — watch for young children here. Cross Yank Way at 1.3 miles onto the Yankee Doodle Greenbelt, a linear park with no playgrounds or facilities. The trail abuts Alkire Ct/Cole Ct momentarily, then dives back into the greenbelt as the gully grows a little wilder and more scenic. A large sign declares "End of Bike Trail" at Deframe St (1.7), but the path continues across the street on the south bank of the creek.

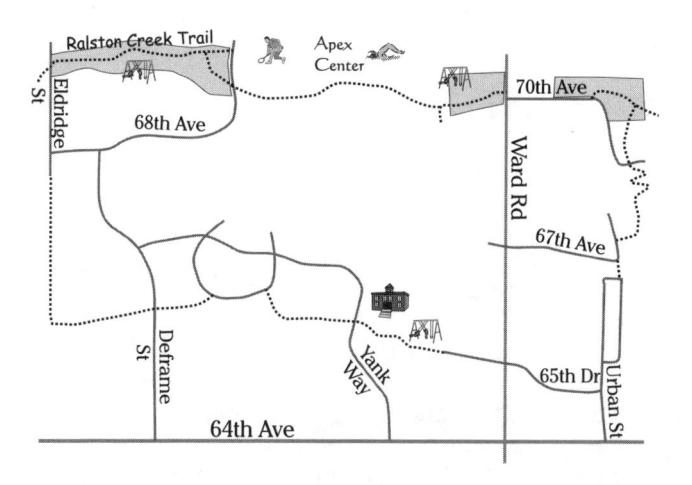

The trail seems to end at the extension of Eldridge St (2.0), but a few yards of dirt connects it to a sidewalk on the 'street that doesn't exist'. Some maps call it 'Eldridge'; instead you'll find a sidewalk, fences, curbs, and a wide path of dirt and grass. Follow the sidewalk past the 'Road Closed' barriers (2.3), where *Eldridge* really begins. Stay on the sidewalk until a path to the right drops into the Ralston Valley Park and connects to the *Ralston Creek Path*.

For a loop trip, you can continue east on the path, passing behind the Apex Center and crossing Ward Rd before hitting the trail junction you started at (4.2). For more details on this trail, see the writeup for the *Ralston Creek Central Trail*.

TRAIL OPTIONS:

From the east end, travel *Ralston Creek Central* toward downtown Arvada. From the west end, *Ralston Creek West* goes another 6.9 miles, ending at Arvada Reservoir.

$\bigvee$ an Bibber Creek Trail and Loop

DISTANCE: *2.3 miles (optional 4.6 mile loop)*

ON-STREET: *difficult crossing of Ward Rd at 56th Dr*

SURFACE: *concrete, dirt/gravel*

DIFFICULTY: *easy-to-moderate; loop has climbing*

DESCRIPTION:

Clear Creek, Ralston Creek, and the Fairmount Canal form a triangle in central Jefferson County, with trails allowing you to do a long loop on the fringes of the area. For the cyclist who wishes to tour a smaller, interior portion of Arvada and unincorporated areas, <u>Van Bibber Open Space Park</u> offers a convenient starting point. You can take a long point-to-point trail, or you can link other trails in an interesting loop.

Our description starts from the Van Bibber Open Space trailhead on Indiana Ave. Follow the concrete trail east through the narrow corridor between homes and private land. Soon the private land ends, and the Open Space Park widens tremendously. Native grasses wave in the breezes, and scattered trees mark the course of tiny Van Bibber Creek (which the trail crosses three times, though it's hard to notice). The concrete trail stays on the north side of the park, climbing one short rise above the creek. A dirt/crushed gravel trail branches to the right at mile 0.5 (see Trail Option), and rejoins this trail nearer the east edge of the park (1.1). Shortly after it rejoins the park, the concrete trail splits and splits again, but all paths lead to the parking lot (1.3).

You could simply return to your starting point on the dirt trail, doing your loop trip within the park. However, the trail does continue east, or you can make a loop with trails to the north. To continue along the creek, head out of the parking lot to Ward Rd. There is no traffic light here, so good luck crossing this busy street onto 56th Dr. Once you get across, the trail starts again quickly (1.5) on your right.

The trail runs through an undistinguished corridor with homes to the right, the creek to the left, and utility towers soaring above you. Bear left at the first fork, which takes you to a junction on the edge of the <u>Stegner Soccer Complex</u> (2.0). If you turn right on the new concrete trail, you will reach a 'T' junction that will take you to 55th Ln (left, 2.2) or 54th Ln (right, 2.3). Instead, head left into the soccer fields. Stay on the south side of the creek to pass through the complex, ending on Oak St (2.5) at the <u>Harold D. Lutz Sports Complex</u>.

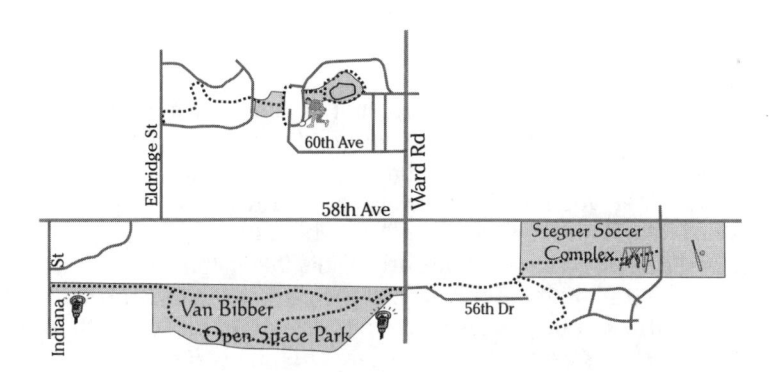

If you're looking for more exertion, forego the sports field for a loop ride. Instead of crossing Ward Rd, stay on the wide sidewalk and head north beside Ward Rd. After crossing 58th Ave, the sidewalk narrows, but stay on it until you hit 60th Ave (1.9). Take a break from climbing as you head west a short ways on *60th*, then turn right on *Wright* or *Xenon St* to finish your ascent. They end on *62nd Ave*, which you turn left onto to reach Meadowlake (2.3).

You can ride either side of this charming pond; I choose the north side. On the east end (2.6), stay north of the tennis court to reach Zinnia St. Turn right, and make an immediate left on 62nd Dr (which says 'no outlet'). At the end, follow the path into the grassy corridor. A right at either of the first two junctions will take you to Wyndham Park. Follow the trail (or the street) to the corner of Wyndham Park & 62nd Dr (3.0).

The concrete trail continues west from this corner, a wide sidewalk through the greenbelt. Don't get confused when it changes to a narrow walkway and veers north to 63rd Ave. When it reaches 63rd, stay on the sidewalk. It will shortly veer right south again, becoming a wide trail once more. Stay on this until you reach Eldridge St, at which our trail ends. To return to Van Bibber, head south on *Eldridge*, turn right (west) on *58th Ave*, and left on *Fig Way*. This street winds around and becomes *56th Dr*, which ends on *Indiana St*. Two quick left turns take you back into Van Bibber Park.

TRAIL OPTION:

When the concrete trail first enters the wide portion of the park (0.5), you can turn right on the dirt/crushed gravel trail. Follow that as it climbs partway up the south ridge. When you hit a junction, follow it down to the left (use your brakes) and follow the trail as it becomes a narrow, raised trail above a wetlands area. This takes you back to the concrete trail on the north side of the park. Note that turning right at the junction takes you to 54th Ave at Alkire St. Another dirt trail heads east in the park at this point, but it can get chewed up – its better to leave it for the equestrians.

Fairmount Trail

DISTANCE: 3.7 miles off-street

ON-STREET: cross Easley Rd

SURFACE: dirt and gravel with sandy spots

DIFFICULTY: moderate

DESCRIPTION:

Cyclists could argue that the best trails in the metro area follow natural waterways. The Platte River Trail and those that follow the numerous creeks provide solid arguments for that position.

However, area canal trails vie for excellence, led (of course) by the Highline Canal through Denver and its southern and eastern suburbs. In northern Jefferson County, the Ralston/Clear Creek Canal snakes along the foothills between Arvada Reservoir and Clear Creek, skirting North Table Mountain. The Fairmount Trail provides access to this scenic area.

The south spur of the trail starts on Salvia Dr, north of 44th Ave (follow signs to the Coors Employee Recreation Center). Park just outside the Rec Center gate, and catch the trail heading west. Be sure to take the trail, not the adjacent private driveway. It starts out a bit sandy as it climbs a very slight slope. Quickly it reaches the edge of the private property, turning north into a tree-lined lane. At mile 0.3 you reach a junction at Golden's off-leash park, with the Fairmount east spur and the north (main) trail. The east spur (heading straight) is described later in this writeup; we'll turn left here.

Cross Easley Rd (watch for traffic, since there is no signal here) onto a narrow dirt path. This rocky path is easier to walk road bikes than ride. Luckily it doesn't last, and you reach the junction with the main trail at mile 0.4. To the south, a trail does continue along the canal, but signs warn that there is no public access. Head north (right) instead on the exposed gravel path. On both sides, distinctive homes (no cracker box developments here!) dot

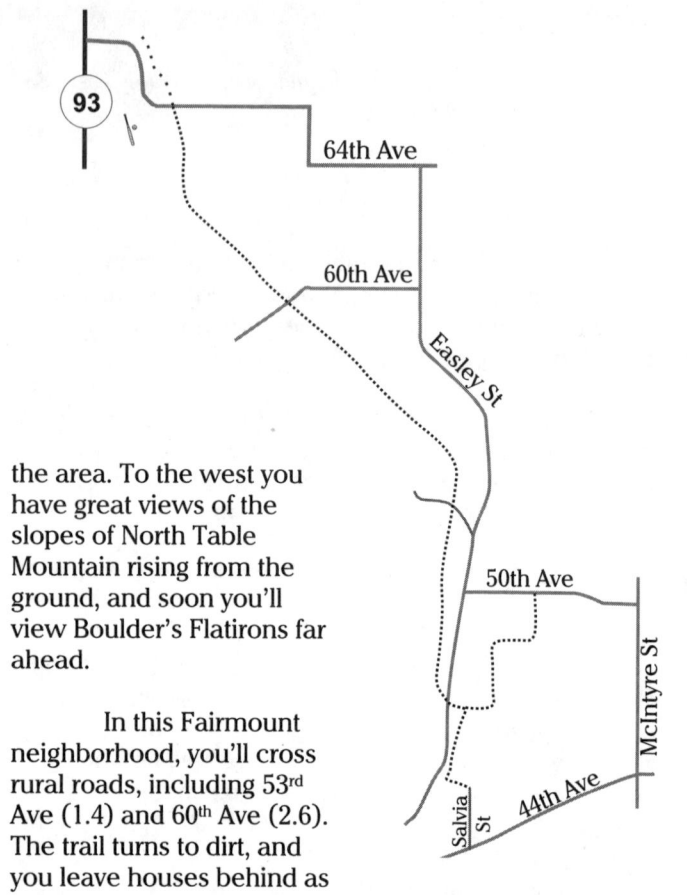

the area. To the west you have great views of the slopes of North Table Mountain rising from the ground, and soon you'll view Boulder's Flatirons far ahead.

In this Fairmount neighborhood, you'll cross rural roads, including 53rd Ave (1.4) and 60th Ave (2.6). The trail turns to dirt, and you leave houses behind as you follow the canal through open fields. The trail grows rougher as you head north, but it remains accessible to road bikes. It ends at mile 3.7, after tunneling under 66th Ave to the *Arvada Reservoir Trail*. Reset your odometer and return along the same route.

To make this trail a semi-loop, leave the trail on your return at *53rd Ave* (2.3). Follow it east (left) to *Easley Rd*, and turn right a short distance to reach *50th Ave* (2.6). Turn left on 50th until you find the east spur opposite Quaker St (2.9). Take the trail south/right (again, be sure not to jump on the

adjacent private road). When the private road crosses the path, continue straight on the sandy path. At mile 3.1 the path hits a new street and promptly turns 90°right. It soon crosses a side canal above the Rec Center, entering the tree-lined area. At mile 3.8 it reaches the south and main spur junction. Continue straight ahead to return to Salvia St (4.1).

TRAIL OPTIONS:

You can cross 66th Ave and hop on the *Arvada Reservoir Trail*. Be forewarned, though – you will quickly hit one of the steepest sections of paved trail in the metro area, climbing the bluff just north of the reservoir.

At the end of the eastern spur of the trail, head east on 50 th Ave to McIntyre St (0.6 miles), and turn south (right) until you cross over CO58 (1.6). Turn left on the frontage road (NOT the freeway on-ramp) and follow it to the trailhead for the *Clear Creek Trail* (1.9).

<u>*OTHER ATTRACTIONS:*</u>

     Golden, with its numerous attractions, lies only a few miles west. Much closer is the COLORADO RAILROAD MUSEUM, just east of Salvia on 44th Ave. This twelve-acre park hosts engines and rail cars you can climb on and in, an exhibition hall with railroad equipment, posters, and maps, and both indoor and outdoor scale model train layouts. Of particular interest are DR&G engine #346, the oldest operating locomotive in Colorado; Big Boy, one of the largest engines ever made; and Galloping Goose #2, a train car built (cannibalized?) with parts from a Buick, a Peirce Arrow, a Ford truck, and a railroad engine.

C*lear Creek Trail central*

DISTANCE: *6.8 miles, 6.6 off-street*

SURFACE: *concrete*

DIFFICULTY: *easy ride*

DESCRIPTION:

One of the premier trails in the Denver area, this ride follows Clear Creek through many well-kept parks and greenbelts in the north Jefferson county area. One important role this trail plays is a connector for several other trails in the area. This central portion of the trail connects the two longest creek trails dumping into this trail: Ralston and Little Dry.

This trail segment begins west of the batting cages on 64th Ave, west of Pecos Blvd. The trail starts where the *Little Dry Creek Trail* merges with it, on the edge of pond reclaimed from a gravel pit. The concrete path heads back toward the creek, passing through an industrial landscape (gravel is still a going business concern here). Thankfully the trees along the creek mostly block one-half of the view.

At mile 1.0 pass under Federal Blvd, meeting a street connection on the west side. Now the trail passes through its lushest area, with trees providing shade. To your right, enjoy a brief moment of relief from the industrial scenery - a farm is raising a small crop. It won't last! The trail next crosses over the creek (1.5) and makes a sharp right turn to pass under the twin lanes of I-76.

The next street that looms is Lowell St. The trail passes under the road, with trailheads and parking on either side. You have reached the Lowell Ponds State Wildlife Refuge! To your left, ponds and open fields provide an oasis for migrating birds. You may enter this area (without your bike) if you're up for birding or just want to relax away from others. The refuge doesn't last long, and soon you reach Tennyson St (2.3). Take care at this crossing, as the cars on the road have no stop sign.

You quickly leave behind the houses to again tunnel under I-76 (2.6). Take heart – there are bound to be drivers stuck on the highway that are envying you right now! The trail is now sandwiched between interstate and quarries as you cross under Sheridan Blvd (2.8). On the west side, you immediately see the spire and cables of the graceful

new bridge over the creek, which marks the start of the *Ralston Creek Trail*. As you continue along the south side of the creek, try to ignore the traffic on I-76 to your left. Once you cross under the freeway (3.2), you have a chance to put them behind you.

The off-street trail ends temporarily at 52nd Ave (3.5). Cross it onto *Gray St*, following that quiet street to its end and then turning right on *Clear Creek Dr.* The trail quickly picks up again on the right (3.7). It now passes through a quiet area bounded on the south by a ridge lined with houses. The next landmark you hit is a new park nestled into the corner carved out as 48th Ave curves to become Marshall St (3.9). This facility boasts baseball diamonds, a playground, and a concrete trail looping around the perimeter.

The trail stays close by the stream, crossing Marshall St, then diving under the I-70/I-76 interchange at mile 4.6.

Trees line the trail on both sides, but it is not enough to break the noise from the steady traffic. After crossing under Wadsworth Blvd (5.0), though, the trail takes on a more restful tone. It starts with <u>Johnson Park</u>, a small jewel of a park with a pond nestled on the creek. Next up: the start of the Wheatridge Greenbelt, another tree-lined area slightly farther removed from houses and highways. Retain that peace as you cross the creek at 5.6 miles.

Cross under 44th Ave at mile 6.0, and skirt <u>Anderson Park</u>. Once again we're traveling through woodlands, though houses border the trail on the right. The unmarked junction at mile 6.5 signals the end of this leg. If you go straight ahead, you reach the <u>Kipling St</u> trailhead at mile 6.7; this is a good place to park if you want to start off riding east.

OPTIONS:

From the eastern end, the remainder of the *Clear Creek Trail* starts directly across the street from the batting cages. (The easiest way to reach it from this segment is to ride up *Little Dry Creek* and turn right at the first junction, riding back by the batting cages. The direct connection is an unimproved 0.1mile path that takes you up the narrow sidewalk, crosses a dirt patch by the railing, crosses the railroad tracks on the street, and drops back to the trail.)

Head left at mile 2.9, crossing over the bridge to begin the *Ralston Creek Trail*. You can also head upstream at the *Little Dry Creek*, ending up close to Standley Lake.

At the western end of the trail, continue under the bridge and follow the *Clear Creek Trail* west to the Coors brewery and into Golden.

Clear Creek Trail west

DISTANCE: *7.7 estimated miles, 7.5 off-street*

ON-STREET: *residential streets*

SURFACE: *concrete*

DIFFICULTY: *easy ride*

DESCRIPTION:

One of the premier trails in the Denver area, this ride follows Clear Creek through many well-kept parks and greenbelts in the north Jefferson county area. As of early 2004, that trail should finally reach all the way into Golden, completing a run of 17 miles from the South Platte River. This makes it second only to Cherry Creek in trail length (and at this time, the two long stretches of that trail are not connected).

We have arbitrarily chosen the 'beginning' of this leg to occur at the Kipling trailhead as a half-way point between Little Dry Creek and Tucker Gulch. You can park here and proceed up- or downstream along the creek path. For the western leg, head east to reach the main trail (0.2 miles), where we will mark mileage from. Turn right over the bridge and exit onto Independence Ct. Quickly turn right on *41st Ave*, then turn left onto the trail before reaching Kipling. It winds south, passes under Kipling, then executes a sharp turn as it rises into the parking lot of the Wheatridge Recreation Center (0.6). Follow the path, watching for traffic in the parking lot, as you work your way north.

The trail dumps you back onto *41st Ave*. Turn left, following the street to its end. It turns to gravel as it drops into a Wheatridge Greenbelt park (0.9). This is another ideal trailhead for this ride, as the off-street trail begins again in this wooded glade.

Slow down as you pass through the trail's wildest area. As you cross the bridge at 1.0 miles, listen to the creek gurgle and the birds sing. The trees thin out as you reach <u>Prospect Park</u> (1.5) and Prospect Lake (1.7), another trail access point with ball fields and restrooms. Tabor Lake comes into view at 1.9 miles and West Lake at 2.2 as you re-cross the creek; both are dug out of a barren landscape. The trail follows the north shore of West Lake until hitting one more trailhead with picnic tables at <u>Youngfield St</u> (2.4 miles).

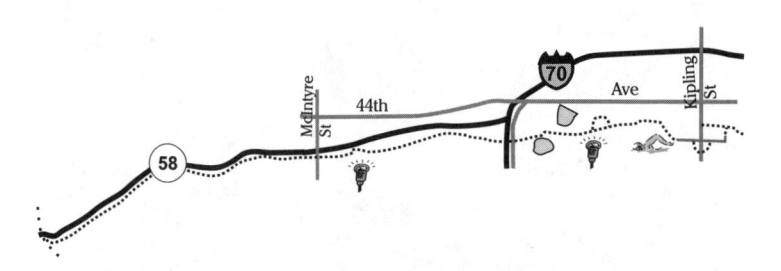

After crossing under Youngfield and I-70, your scenery options are a quarry to the south or the barren boulder-filled creek to the north. The trail crosses Clear Creek one last time, then runs through a narrow gap between the fenced-in Coors Fire Training Center and the busy highway CO-58. At mile 3.8 trees provide a buffer, but by then it's nearly too late to enjoy them. The trail reaches another trailhead at mile 4.1, just shy of the McIntyre St exit from the highway.

For years, this served as the western terminus of the trail. In late 2003, though, Jefferson County began extending the trail into Golden (completion expected in spring 2004). The extension starts as a concrete ribbon running between the highway guardrail and a chain-link fence. The surrounding grounds were relegated to dirt during construction, but will likely be landscaped (which will take time to mature). At mile 5.5, you start climbing beside the railing to cross over 44th Ave. The highway we were following, CO58, is far above us now. The last stretch of trail (under construction at press time) meanders between 44th

Ave and the highway, with views of North Table Mountain on your right. The trail will end at *Tucker Gulch*, dumping into that trail as it passes under CO58.

OPTIONS:

From the eastern end, continue east on this trail. Eventually you can connect all the way to the *Platte River Trail*.

At the McIntyre St trailhead, exit the trail and follow the frontage road west 0.3 miles. Turn north (right) on *McIntyre*, taking it north to 50th Ave (1.3). Head west on *50th* until you reach the end of the eastern spur of the *Fairmount Trail* (1.9).

OTHER ATTRACTIONS:

The brand-new Wheatridge Recreation Center is located on the trail at Kipling Street. This facility joins the growing ranks of municipal rec centers with pools, indoor basketball and racquetball, and classes.

Twice a day, Stephany's Chocolates (6670 W 52nd Ave) offers 45-minute tours of its new factory in Arvada. What more needs to be said? Call 303-421-7229 x111.

If you're interested in early Wheatridge, visit the Wheatridge Historic Park (4610 Robb St). Among the buildings on the grounds is an 1860s sod house (now a museum with furninshings reflecting farm life late in the 19th century); a five-room brick bungalow from 1892; a log cabin (circa 1863) built by one of the Colorado Territory's first homesteaders; and Wheatridge's first post office, dating from 1913. Call 303-421-9111.

Golden City Loop

DISTANCE: 3.8 mile loop, 2.9 miles off-street

SURFACE: concrete

DIFFICULTY: moderate ride with one steep climb

DESCRIPTION:

Golden will, perhaps, be forever known as 'the Home of Coors Beer'. However, this little town nestled in the foothills of the Rockies is striving to make a name for itself in recreation circles. Addition of a kayak course on Clear Creek as it tumbles from the canyon has spread the town's name around the country's whitewater circles. For those interested in staying dry, the city also hosts growing miles of bike paths.

This particular ride uses quiet side streets to 'close the loop' on a trip anchored by paved trails. From <u>Vanover Park</u> northeast of downtown, cross over the side stream on the wooden bridge and head left or north (the southside spur ends quickly at a Coors parking lot). You climb steadily if not steeply, and the concrete-bordered creek to your side ascends in a series of steps. (If you're lucky, you may actually see water in it.) Take this concrete path through the commercial landscape until you cross under CO53 at mile 0.3. (There should be a connection to the east-bound *Clear Creek Trail* here in spring 2004, but this trail may be closed during that construction.)

Cross 7th Pl as the path (the Tucker Gulch Trail) enters a residential section. You still climb steadily as you proceed up the greenbelt, and trees provide intermittent shade. To your right, houses extend to the base of North Table Mountain. In Mesa Meadows Park, the trail branches (mile 0.7), with the straight ahead spur leading you to 1st St. Instead, take the hairpin turn sharply down (grab your brakes!) to cross over the creek, then continue climbing up the creek's west bank.

The next stretch of trail offers stunning views of Golden's trademark butte to the east. (Anyone up for a John Wayne movie?) Enjoy the last bit of climbing and greenbelt, as you reach the end of the Tucker Gulch Trail at mile 1.1. Now comes time to navigate city streets! Head left onto *Ford St*, biking to the stop sign at Iowa St (do not be confused by Iowa Dr or Iowa Ct on your left). Turn right on *Iowa St* (1.4), and take that through the light at Washington Ave (1.5). Turn left onto the next street (*Rubey Dr*, 1.6).

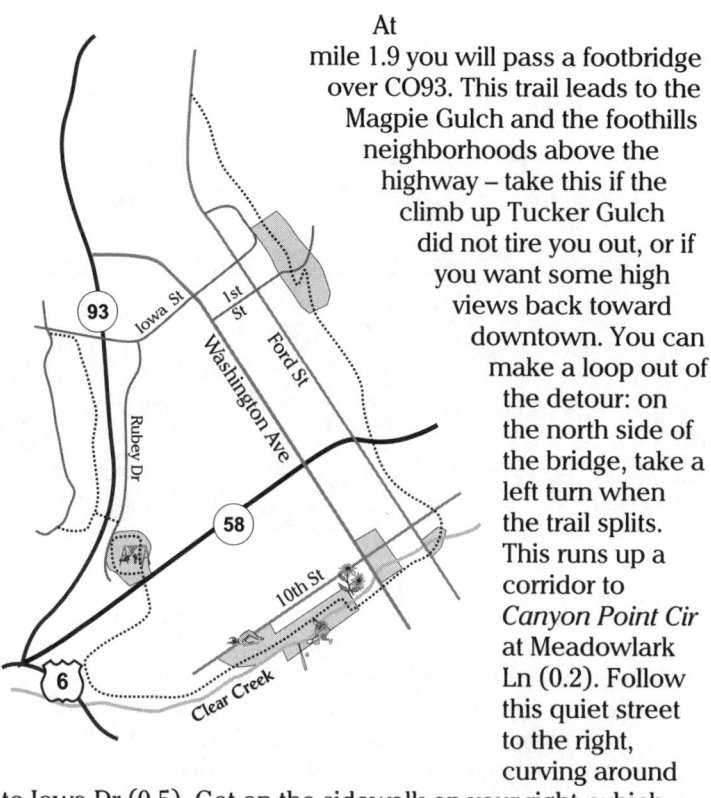

At mile 1.9 you will pass a footbridge over CO93. This trail leads to the Magpie Gulch and the foothills neighborhoods above the highway – take this if the climb up Tucker Gulch did not tire you out, or if you want some high views back toward downtown. You can make a loop out of the detour: on the north side of the bridge, take a left turn when the trail splits. This runs up a corridor to *Canyon Point Cir* at Meadowlark Ln (0.2). Follow this quiet street to the right, curving around to Iowa Dr (0.5). Get on the sidewalk on your right, which curves into the grassy buffer just below the tract as it curves back to the bridge you originally crossed. You've now added 0.8 miles to your ride!

Farther down Rubey from the bridge, you'll reach the <u>New Loveland Mine Park</u> at High Point Dr & 5th St (2.1). Turn left and enter the park by a port-a-potty and playground. The sidewalks on either side of the park join on the far side, and the path drops steeply with a switchback as it heads to a bridge over highway CO58. (Take a moment to read the interpretive sign describing the New Loveland mine, which produced coal in the 1880s and '90s.)

On the far side of the highway (2.5), follow the trail by the canal, which reaches the creek at mile 2.8. Turn left to follow the concrete creekside path as it travels beside an RV park, then enters Golden's recreation cradle. Across the street lies the <u>Golden Community Center</u>, and you pass by <u>Lions Park</u> with tennis courts and fields for organized sports. To your right, kayakers challenge the slalom course in the rushing creek. Cross over the bridge at mile 3.3 – staying straight takes you past the Golden Museum and the small President's Rose Garden before ending at Washington St.

On the south side of the creek, the trail splits again. The right branch ends quickly at 11th St & Illinois St. To the left, the trail passes an outdoor museum before burrowing under Washington. A bit further on it bridges the creek, delivering you back to Vanover Park (3.8), where we started.

<u>OTHER ATTRACTIONS:</u>

When people think of Golden, Coors usually comes to mind. The Coors Brewery has put (and kept) Golden on the map, as they transform Rocky Mountain spring water into one of America's favorite beverages. Every year 350,000 sign up for the half-hour tour. You can check out the 13,000 gallon copper kettles, the malting department, or see the bottles and cans racing along the conveyor belts. And save up your thirst – the tasting room awaits you at the end of the tour.

Looking for history to enliven your present? You can visit the Golden Pioneer Museum (923 10th St), which tells the story of Golden and environs from pioneers through WWII. (You can view Golden's first galvanized bathtub!) Call 303-278-7151. If you'd like to step into the past, check out the Clear Creek History Park (11th & Arapahoe Sts). Here, costumed interpreters recreate late-19th- and early-20th-century life, leading tours through the 1876 Guy Hill School, 1870s log cabins, a blacksmith's shop, barn, and more. This park is run by the Friends of Astor House (822 12th St), a museum located in a former hotel that catered to the elite in Golden, Colorado's former territorial capital. Call 303-278-3557.

Other museums in town focus on narrow specialties. For more Alpine interests, the American Mountaineering Museum (710 10th St) houses the US flag carried atop Mt Whitney in 1865, a scale model of Mt Everest, and 18,000 volumes of mountaineering books. This former junior high school building is shared by the American Alpine Club, the Colorado Mountain Club, and the Colorado Outward Bound School. Call 303-384-0110. If your pursuits run toward the more passive, you can learn about the history and art of quilts and quilt-making at the Rock Mountain Quilt Museum (1111 Washington Ave). The museum, with over 200 quilts on-site, is one of only six museums nation-wide dedicated to quilting. Call 303-277-0377.

Art lovers, Golden hasn't forgotten you. The Foothills Art Center (809 15th St) runs an annual theme show, self-curated exhibitions, and juried exhibitions (including competitions in clay, watermedia, and sculpture). The center's six galleries are housed in an 1872 church building and adjacent Victorian mansion. Call 303-279-3922.

The outdoors also calls. Northwest of town, Golden Gate Canyon State Park (3873 Golden Gate Cyn Rd) covers 14,000 acres with 35 miles of hiking trails, 15 miles of mountain bike trails, and a visitor center with exhibits on area history, wildlife, weather, geology, and recreational opportunities. Call 303-582-3707.

K*inney Run Trail*

DISTANCE: *1.9 miles off-street*

SURFACE: *concrete*

DIFFICULTY: *nice workout heading uphill (to the south)*

DESCRIPTION:

You don't need a long creek in order to plot a trail beside it. Though many well-known trails (Boulder Creek, Clear Creek, Bear Creek) run for miles beside waterways that drain the foothills, there are more less-famous paths that run for a mile or two along feeder creeks. Though the distances you can ride along these tributaries pales compared to the main trails, you can often gain the benefit of a steeper, more challenging ride. A case in point is the new Kinney Run Trail in Golden.

I'll describe this trail in the easy, downhill direction. (If you're looking for a good workout, simply reverse these directions.) You can find the south end of this ride at the northern edge of the Heritage Square parking lot. After crossing the wooden bridge, you will immediately pass the junction of the footpath/mountain biking Apex Trail. If you're into cross-training, you can take an enjoyable hike into the foothills above Heritage Square.

Our cement bike trail heads south here, climbing slightly to a crest (0.1) where you can look out on South Table Mountain. Now you start the downhill run! After crossing Kimball Ave (0.3) – be sure to watch for traffic – views into Golden's urban valley open up. The trail itself runs through a groomed park corridor between houses.

The trail soon grows steep, dropping into Heritage Dell Park. Pass the connection that runs back to Crawford St, and ride through the park. On the far side, a dirt 'road' between Shelton Elementary School (to the west) and

Somerset Dr (east) provides a park boundary. Below this, the gulch becomes more a ravine, with houses on the east perched atop sandstone cliffs bordering the trail.

Take the bridge over the creek (0.7), and the trail then quickly dumps you onto the street. Turn west onto *Tripp Dr*, head north (right) immediately on *Crawford*, and then take a quick right onto *Tripp Rd*. This road is marked as a 'private drive', but is open for bicycles to access the lower portion of the Kinney Run Trail (0.9).

The lower portion of the gulch still offers towering sandstone cliffs to your right, while the canyon walls to the left melt away and fill with homes. Here more bushes and trees line the creek. You finally leave this subdivision behind by passing beneath Eagleridge Dr (1.3). (There are connectors to the street here.) To the north, the cliffs soon disappear, leaving you with views of the traffic on US6. Luckily for us, the trail passes under that traffic (1.6), emerging on the north side to merge with the new *US6 Trail* (1.7).

Though that is the end of the Kinney Run Trail, you can extend this ride further towards Golden proper. Turn right (southeast) on the US6 trail, then take a left at the next junction (1.8). This side trail climbs a short distance through a newly landscaped (as of late 2003) hillside, then coasts down to end behind the local waterpark (2.0).

U*S6 Trail*

DISTANCE: *2.5 miles off-street*

SURFACE: *concrete*

DIFFICULTY: *up and down short hills*

DESCRIPTION:

The jewels of the metro area trail network lie along the numerous waterways, giving the rider a chance to reconnect with nature. However, 'network' implies a multitude of trails connecting with each other. Since creeks and canals are not always placed conveniently to make those connections, we must rely on trails between housing tracts or (often) beside major highways to get from point to point.

The US6 trail is a fine example of such a path. Paralleling the thoroughfare between 19th St and Golden Rd, this path does not offer shade trees or babbling brooks. It does, however knit together different sections of town, allowing the rider to escape the city streets. Connecting the ends of this path with a very few miles of street riding, you can ride a loop through the metropolitan area of 40+ miles, 65 miles, or more.

This trail starts in the north at the corner of US6 & 19th St. You start off riding through an area with trees, crossing a 'bridge' over a trickling stream, and climbing slightly to a crest (0.4). Now the trail slopes downward. It alternates between hiding below the highway embankment and looking down on the highway. Take heart that you're not fighting that traffic!

You'll reach the Kinney Run Gulch at mile 0.8, which hosts the *Kinney Run Trail*. If you'd like a serious workout, branch right on this trail and climb to Heritage Square. Our trail bears left, passing another side trail (0.9) leading to a

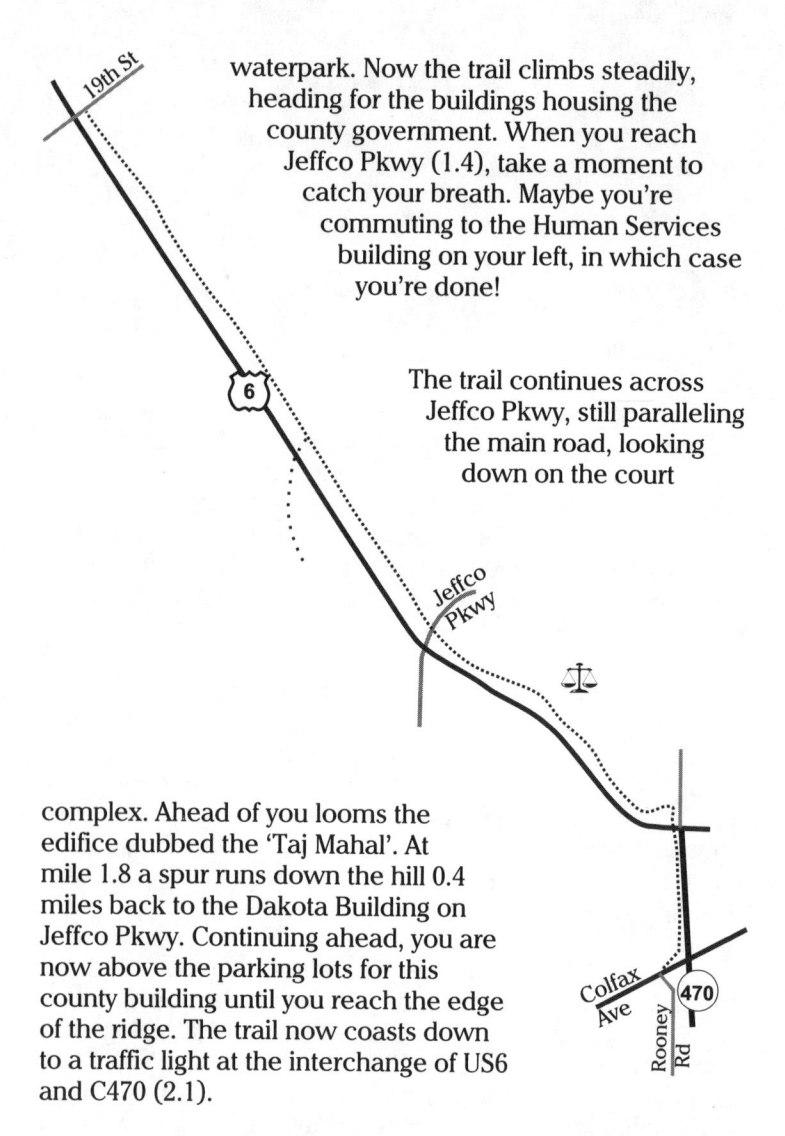

waterpark. Now the trail climbs steadily, heading for the buildings housing the county government. When you reach Jeffco Pkwy (1.4), take a moment to catch your breath. Maybe you're commuting to the Human Services building on your left, in which case you're done!

The trail continues across Jeffco Pkwy, still paralleling the main road, looking down on the court

complex. Ahead of you looms the edifice dubbed the 'Taj Mahal'. At mile 1.8 a spur runs down the hill 0.4 miles back to the Dakota Building on Jeffco Pkwy. Continuing ahead, you are now above the parking lots for this county building until you reach the edge of the ridge. The trail now coasts down to a traffic light at the interchange of US6 and C470 (2.1).

The trail now crosses US6 and leaves that highway behind. It runs south beside the entrance ramp to the C470 freeway. As the road rises to cross over I-70, the trail curves over and runs to Colfax Ave, and then turns right to end at the light at Rooney Rd (2.5).

TRAIL OPTION:

You can head up the *Kinney Run Trail* for a nice exercise ride. Prepare to breathe hard!

OTHER ATTRACTIONS:

One of the oldest museums in Colorado, the Colorado School of Mines Geology Museum (16th & Maple Sts) showcases collections on minerology, paleontology, geology, and Colorado mining, including exhibits on minerals and gems. They also offer tours of the Edgar Experimental Mine, an underground classroom/laboratory in Idaho Springs. Call 303-273-3815.

Closer to the city, the Lookout Mountain Nature Center (910 Colorow Rd) hosts nature exhibits, programs, and lectures, as well as serving as a jumping-off point for its 8.5 miles of hiking trails. They also tailor programs for children of many ages. Call 303-526-0694. Next door to the center, the 1917 Boetcher Mansion (900 Colorow Rd), the summer home and hunting lodge of Charles Boetcher, contains arts-and-crafts style furnishings and information on Lookout Mountain and Golden. Call 303-526-0855.

You've seen the signs; now visit the site! The Mother Cabrini Shrine on Lookout Mountain (20189 Cabrini Blvd) honors Frances Xavier Cabrini, the first US saint. You may have seen the 22' statue of the Sacred Heart while you zipped by on I-70, but there is also a 1915 stone house and barn, a prayer building, chapel, convent, and gift shop. Call 303-526-0758.

South Golden Rd Trail

DISTANCE: 1.1 miles off-street

SURFACE: concrete

DIFFICULTY: easy to moderate ride

DESCRIPTION:

This book may be full of wonderful recreational rides, but this ride is not one of them. It doesn't cut through a wildlife area; it doesn't follow a scenic stream; it doesn't run for miles. What it does is provide the rider with an escape from traffic on city streets on a trip between the heart of town and its southern reaches. It can also be combined with city streets (some busy, some not) and part of the US6 trail for a loop trip, if you are so inclined.

This trail essentially parallels South Golden Rd from its beginning south to Ulysses St. You may pick up this concrete path just beyond the point where Ford and Jackson Sts merge. The trail runs up the west side of the road, climbing slowly in the broad open-space belt that separates the wetland and golf course from the road. You're never far from traffic, but maybe if you keep looking across the golf greens on the west, you won't notice.

At mile 0.5 you reach the first traffic circle. Cross Earle Johnson Rd, continuing to head south beside SG Rd. A retail strip mall has replaced the golf course on your right, so be cautious of traffic in or out. When you hit the next traffic circle (0.7), relief is on the way. Follow the trail branching to your right, taking you away from SG Rd. The path angles up the hillside behind the strip businesses and fast food emporiums (I hope you weren't hungry, because the smell of cooking grease may start you salivating.)

At least on the hillside you have a bit of nature surrounding you. The path runs through an edge of Ulysses

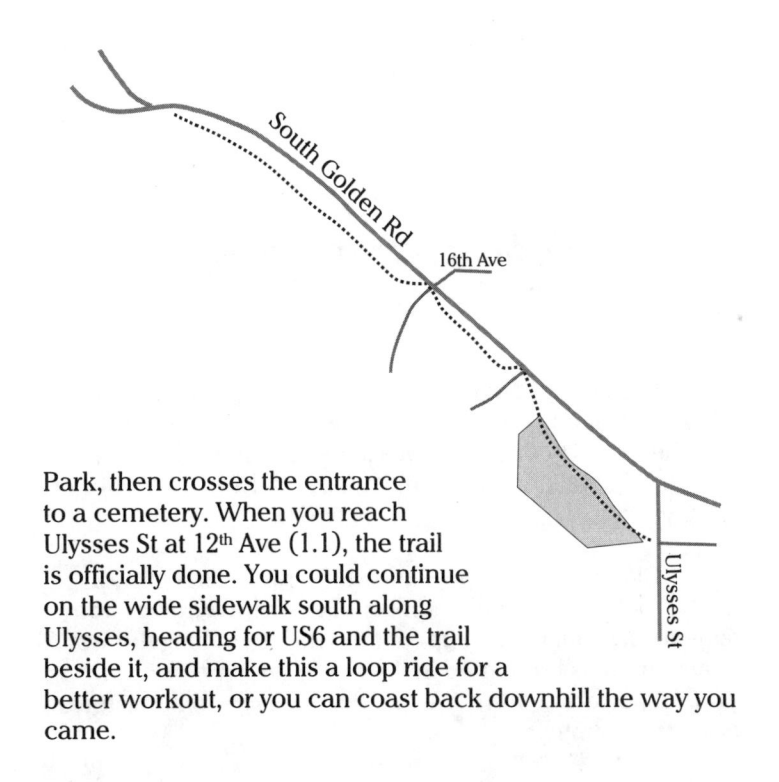

Park, then crosses the entrance
to a cemetery. When you reach
Ulysses St at 12th Ave (1.1), the trail
is officially done. You could continue
on the wide sidewalk south along
Ulysses, heading for US6 and the trail
beside it, and make this a loop ride for a
better workout, or you can coast back downhill the way you
came.

About the Author --

Glen Hanket was raised in Boulder, Colorado when it was still a sleepy college town. A software engineer by trade, he writes books and gives speeches and slide shows on bicycling, walking, National Parks, and the evils of litter in his 'spare time.'

Glen is perhaps best known for his LitterWalk -- a hike he took with his wife (shortly after their wedding) from Maine to Oregon, picking up four tons of litter along the way. His adventure is recounted in the book, *Underwear by the Roadside*, available from CAK Publishing or from bookstores across the country.

You may order any of our fine bicycle trail guides on the web at www.bikepaths.com. You can also use the convenient order form below.

Please send me:

Underwear by the Roadside ($10.00) _____
Trails Away Colorado ($10.00) _____
Take A Bike! 2nd edition ($12.95) _____
from 2001 *Take A Bike!* Series ($6.50 each)
   Jefferson County South Urban Trails _____
   Denver/Platte Triangle Urban Trails _____
   Aurora/East Metro Urban Trails _____
   Douglas County Urban Trails _____
new 2004 *Take A Bike!* Series ($7.00 each)
   Boulder Urban Trails _____
   Broomfield/Boulder County Urban Trails _____
   Adams County Urban Trails _____
   Westminster Urban Trails _____
   Jefferson County Central Urban Trails _____
   Northern Colorado Urban Trails _____
   Mountain Resorts Urban Trails _____

I am enclosing the specified amount (less 10% for orders of 2 books or more), plus shipping and handling of $1.50 for one book/$2.25 for two books/$3.00 for 3 or more books. Colorado residents, please add 3% tax. Send check or money order to:
   CAK Publishing
   PO Box 953
   Broomfield, CO 80038
Allow up to three weeks for delivery.

SHIP TO: _____

AT: _____

CITY/STATE: _____

                   ZIP: _____